Environment

DEBORAH ELLIOTT

Wayland

Titles in the Into Europe series
include:

Energy
Environment
Farming
Transport

Picture Acknowledgements
Ecoscene 12 (Sally Morgan), 20 (left, Peter Hulme), 22 (Harwood), 25 (top, Sally Morgan), 28 (Hawkes) 34 (Adrian Morgan), 37 (Cooper), 42 (Gryniewicz); Eye Ubiquitous 26 (Eva Miessler), 33 (Derek Redfern), 35 (David Cumming); Greenpeace 15 (Vaccari), 40 (right), 41 (Ferraris); ICCE 32 (Mike Hoggett); Tony Stone Worldwide contents page (Michael Busselle), 5 (Robert Frerck), 9 (John Darling), 10 (Thomas Zimmermann), 11, 16 (Bob Torrez), 18, 27 (Joseph Pobereskin), 30 (Cherville), 40 (left), 43 (Oldrich Karasek), 44 (Jacques Guilloreau); Topham Picture Library 13, 23; Wayland Picture Library 19, 20 (right); Zefa 6, 10 (M. Nissen), 25 (bottom), 29 (F.R. Damm), 36 (Reinhard). All artwork is by Malcolm Walker.

Designed by Malcolm Walker

Text based on *Europe and the Environment* in the Europe series published in 1991.

First published in 1993 by Wayland (Publishers) Limited
61 Western Road, Hove, East Sussex BN3 1JD

British Library Cataloguing in Publication Data
Elliott, Deborah
    Environment. - (Into Europe Series)
    I. Title II. Series
    333.7

ISBN 0 7502 0775 2

Typeset by Kudos
Printed and bound by G.Canale & C.S.p.A. in Turin, Italy

Contents

Environment in danger

The environment is the world around us – plants, animals, rivers, mountains, rocks and oceans.

Europe's environment is in great danger. Farming, industry, transport, fishing, poaching and burning fuels for energy are causing pollution, destroying land and buildings and killing wildlife.

▼ *Some of the dangers facing Europe's environment.*

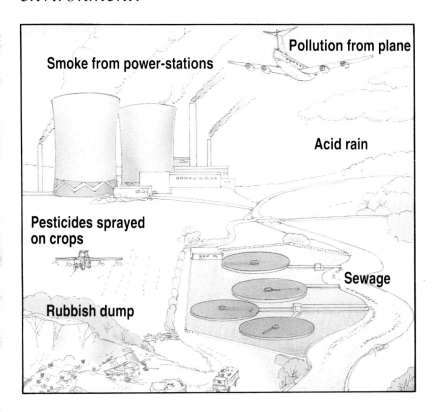

Smoke from power-stations

Pollution from plane

Acid rain

Pesticides sprayed on crops

Sewage

Rubbish dump

▲ *One day motorways, railway lines or factories could replace these green rolling fields in Andalucia in Spain.*

Europe's environment has some of the most beautiful countryside, beaches, mountains and rivers in the world. It also provides food, clothes and homes for the people living in Europe.

Day by day, the threat to the environment grows stronger. What can we do?

Farming

▲ *These lemons have been sprayed with chemicals.*

There are more people living in Europe now than ever before. Farmers in Europe are having to produce more food to feed them.

Many farmers spray their fields with fertilizers. These contain chemicals that make crops grow faster and larger. However, rain sometimes washes the chemicals into rivers and ponds where they cause pollution.

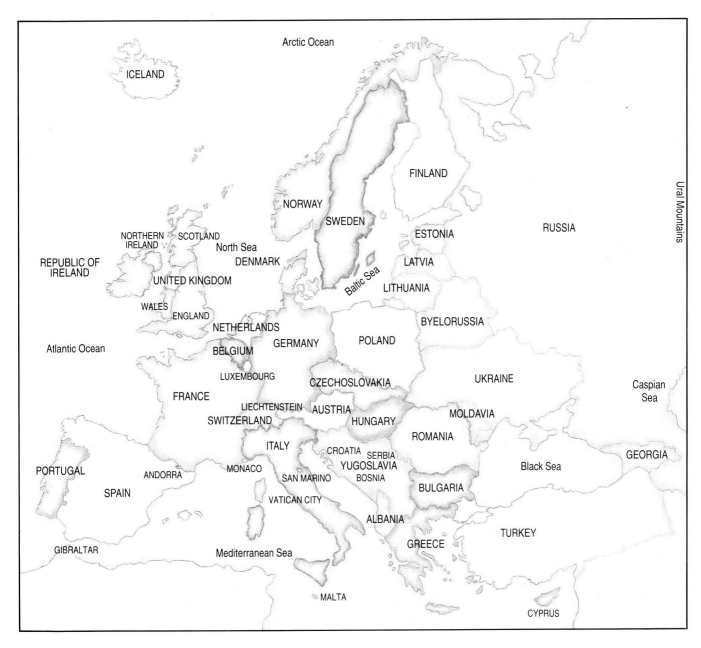

▲ *The countries of Europe.*

Many farmers in Europe also spray their crops with poisonous chemicals called pesticides. They kill the insects that feed on the crops. However, people can become ill if they breathe in the powerful chemicals.

It would be much better for the environment if farmers put natural manure, such as cow dung, on their crops instead of fertilizers.

Farmers could also use ladybirds to eat up insects living on their crops rather than spraying pesticides.

Many countries in southern Europe, such as Spain, Italy and Portugal, are hot and dry and do not get much rain.

Farmers water their crops with rain-water. Rain-water is collected and stored in wells or trenches under the ground. The water then passes along pipes to fields of crops. This is called irrigation farming.

However, sometimes irrigated water leaves a layer of harmful salt on top of the soil. The salt kills the crops.

In the past, farmers changed the type of crop they grew in their fields every couple of years. They also left their fields without any crops for one in every four years. This is called crop rotation. It helps to keep the soil healthy.

Today, farmers do not use crop rotation. Fields are used to grow the same crops year after year. The soil becomes overused and is worn away or destroyed.

Soil can also be blown away by the wind or washed away by rain. This is called soil erosion.

The top layer of soil has been lost from this piece of land in southern Italy. The land has become dry and hard. Nothing can grow on it any more. ▶

This diagram shows some of the ways farmers can look after the soil in their fields. ▶

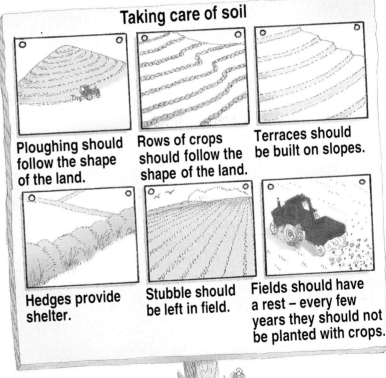

Taking care of soil

Ploughing should follow the shape of the land.

Rows of crops should follow the shape of the land.

Terraces should be built on slopes.

Hedges provide shelter.

Stubble should be left in field.

Fields should have a rest – every few years they should not be planted with crops.

Energy

▲ *Smoke from this power-station is billowing out into the atmosphere, polluting the air we breathe.*

Most industries in Europe use coal, oil or gas as fuel to make electricity. They are burned in power-stations. Smoke from power-stations and factory chimneys contains a chemical called sulphur. This pollutes moisture in the air and makes it acid.

If it is windy, the moisture is blown hundreds of kilometres. Then it falls to the ground as acid rain.

▲ *These trees were once lush and green. Now they are dead – killed by acid rain.*

Acid rain kills trees, crops, plants and fish in rivers and streams. It also pollutes water and destroys buildings.

Coal

When it is burned, coal gives off smoke and ash. These contain a chemical called sulphur and a gas called carbon dioxide.

Sulphur causes acid rain, which kills plants and forests and destroys buildings (see page 11).

Carbon dioxide also harms the environment. The air around the Earth is warmed by heat from the Sun. This heat escapes back into space. However, some gases, such as carbon dioxide, stop the heat from escaping. They trap heat in the way that glass traps heat in a greenhouse. This means the Earth is getting warmer. It is called the greenhouse effect.

◀ *Lignite is burned at this power-station in the east of Germany. Lignite is a brown coal which gives off poisonous gases when burned.*

◀ *Acid rain has worn away the stonework of the Rheims Cathedral in France.*

Many countries in Europe are trying to find ways to stop pollution from acid rain. Filters have been put into the chimneys in some power-stations. These take out the sulphur that causes acid rain.

◀ *Industries in Greece mostly use the brown coal lignite as fuel. You can see the five main lignite mines in Greece on this map.*

Smoke from lignite contains gases which harm the environment.

BULGARIA

YUGOSLAVIA

ALBANIA

Kavalla

Thessalonika

Ptolemais

Kozani

GREECE

TURKEY

Athens

Lignite fields in Greece

Some industries in Europe use nuclear energy to produce electricity in power-stations.

Nuclear energy does not cause acid rain or add to the greenhouse effect. Nuclear energy is powerful rays of energy called radiation. Radiation can be very dangerous if not treated properly.

Waste from nuclear power-stations can harm people, animals and the environment.

▼ *This is Sellafield, a nuclear power-station in the north of England. Many countries in Europe send nuclear waste to Sellafield to be re-used.*

◄ *This cloud of thick, black smoke is from burning oil in the Mediterranean Sea.*

Explosions on oil platforms or oil tankers (ships that carry oil) do not happen often. When they do, however, millions of tonnes of oil is spilled into the sea. This pollutes the water and kills fish, seals and birds. Penguins' feathers become clogged with oil.

It costs huge sums of money to clean up the sea after an oil spill. But the cost to the environment is much greater.

People are trying to find other types of energy which do not harm the environment. These are called types of alternative energy.

▲ *Cleaning up the sea-shore after an oil spill.*

Power from water is called hydroelectric power.

Water from lakes and dams passes through pipes to a hydroelectric (HEP) power-station. The force of the water turns machines which make electricity.

Although hydroelectric power causes very little pollution, it can affect the environment. HEP stations need water from lakes and dams. Sometimes these have to be specially built in areas where many plants and animals live.

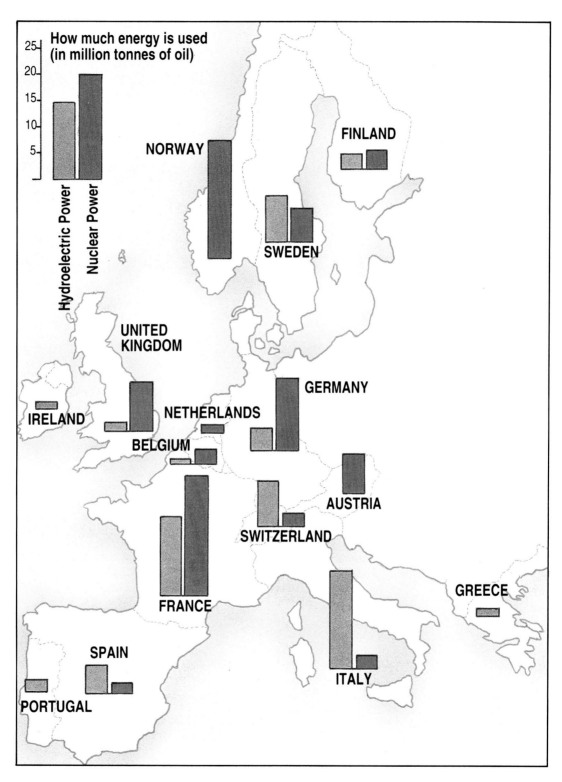

How much energy is used
(in million tonnes of oil)

25
20
15
10
5

Hydroelectric Power

Nuclear Power

NORWAY

FINLAND

SWEDEN

UNITED
KINGDOM

IRELAND

NETHERLANDS

GERMANY

BELGIUM

AUSTRIA

SWITZERLAND

GREECE

FRANCE

SPAIN

ITALY

PORTUGAL

▲ *This map shows how much hydroelectric power and nuclear power is used in Europe.*

Industry

▼ *Many forests in Europe have been planted with conifer trees. These grow very quickly all year round. Once grown the trees are cut down and used for timber.*

▲ *It is important that areas of woodland are looked after.*

Conifer trees are a good supply of timber for industry. However, very few plants, insects, birds or animals can live in them. Conifer trees are planted in very long rows. They make the landscape dark and gloomy.

In Britain, an organization called the Forestry Commission is trying to find more interesting ways to plant conifer trees which will be better for the environment.

Flow Country

Golden eagles (right) have lived in the wild marshes of the Flow Country in north-east Scotland (below) for many years. Sadly these beautiful birds are being driven away by a lack of food.

In the 1980s, about one-third of the area was drained of water. Rows of conifer trees were planted on land which was once home to rabbits, deer and sheep. These animals were food for Golden eagles.

Ireland

Every year people from all over the world visit the lush green countryside of Ireland. The country is known to have one of the cleanest environment's in the world.

Now Ireland's environment is under threat. Lead and zinc have been found in different parts of Ireland. These are valuable minerals which could bring money and jobs to the country.

The lead and zinc are found deep withing the Earth. Huge machines dig up large amounts of rock and land, destroying the soil. Also, dust from lead causes pollution and kills animals.

Large sums of money have been spent making sure that the air and water around some lead and zinc mines do not become polluted.

◀ *These fields have been cut up to provide peat. Peat is used as fuel in the power-station at Shannon Bridge in Ireland.*

▶ *The growth of most babies in Cracow is affected by pollution from the steel factory nearby.*

Many people in southern Poland work in the steel industry. Pollution from the steel factories has poisoned the air, water and food. It has even caused some people to die early.

The town of Cracow is covered in a cloud of black poisonous fog for up to 135 days every year. This is caused by pollution from the nearby steel factory.

The air around the factory is very thick. Most of the babies and young children in Cracow have problems with their health and breathing. These illnesses are caused by pollution from the steel factory.

If the factory closes down, 100,000 people will lose their jobs. Nevertheless, the people of Cracow want the factory to be closed.

The River Rhine is one of the most important rivers in Europe.

Many factories have been built alongside the Rhine. Waste from the factories is dumped in the river.

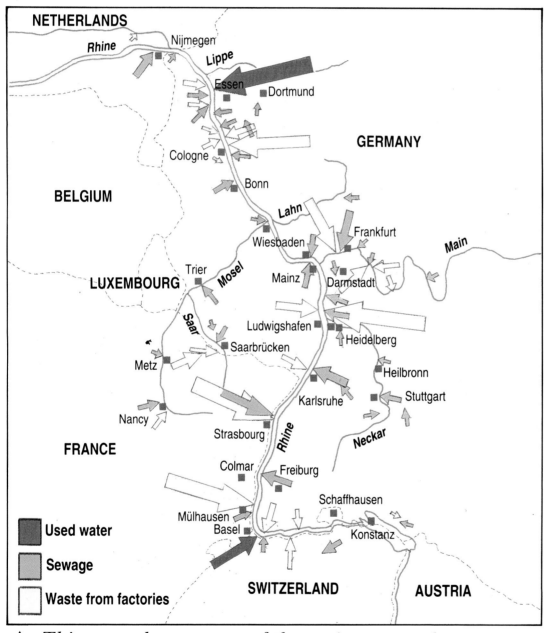

▲ *This map shows some of the main areas where waste is dumped along the River Rhine.*

▲ *Factories are often built alongside rivers. The water is used to cool down machinery. Often, however, waste from the factories is dumped in the rivers.*

◀ *Waste from factories pollutes rivers, killing fish and plants. This photograph was taken on the bank of the River Rhine. Do you think waste should be dumped in rivers?*

There are more factories in Europe now than ever before. This means there is a lot more waste being dumped in Europe's rivers. This is carried along to lakes and seas.

Fish are dying. Drinking water is polluted. It is no longer safe to swim in rivers or lakes, or in much of the sea around Europe.

Many European countries have tried to clean up their rivers. Industries are being made to pay large sums of money if they dump waste in a river without making sure it is safe first.

▼ *The water in this river has been dyed green in order to find out where the pollution has come from.*

Transport and rubbish bins

▲ *Fumes from car exhausts cause pollution. They can hurt our eyes, give us headaches and make it hard to breathe.*

◀ *This road sign is found at traffic lights in Switzerland. It tells drivers to turn off their car engines when the lights are red.*

When car engines are turned off, fumes do not come out of their exhausts.

Ordinary petrol contains very small amounts of lead. Lead is very poisonous and can make people ill if they breathe it in. More and more drivers are using unleaded petrol.

Fumes from vehicle exhausts can be cleaned before they even reach the air. A machine called a catalytic converter can be put into exhaust pipes. This makes most of the poisonous fumes harmless.

Noise pollution also harms the environment. Loud noise from aeroplanes, engines, machines or factories can damage our ears. Some vehicles, such as cars and motor cycles, are fitted with special machines called silencers. These cut down the amount of noise the engines make.

▼ *Aeroplanes get us where we want to go quickly and easily. However, airports cause a lot of noise pollution.*

People who live on busy roads or close to motorways also suffer from noise pollution. Many have double- or even triple-glazed windows. These windows have two or three layers of glass which help to keep the noise out.

Where do you think this photograph was taken? A rubbish dump, perhaps?

It may surprise you to know that it was taken on one of Europe's beaches. The rubbish was washed up from the sea. ▶

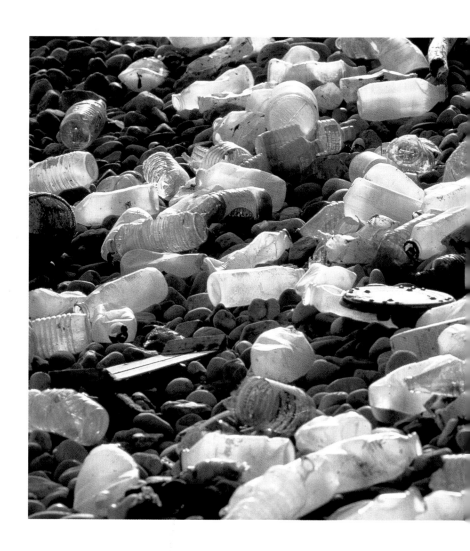

	Amount of waste each year	Amount of waste per person
Norway	1,700,000 tonnes	415 kg
Denmark	2,046,000 tonnes	399 kg
Netherlands	5,400,000 tonnes	381 kg
Germany	20,780,000 tonnes	337 kg
Switzerland	2,146,000 tonnes	336 kg
Belgium	3,082,000 tonnes	313 kg
Sweden	2,500,000 tonnes	300 kg
Finland	1,200,000 tonnes	290 kg
France	15,500,000 tonnes	288 kg
Britain	15,816,000 tonnes	282 kg
Britain	15,816,000 t0nnes	282 kg
Italy	14,041,000 tonnes	246 kg
Spain	8, 028,000 tonnes	214 kg

◀ *This chart shows how much rubbish is thrown away by countries in the European Community (EC).*

The EC is an organization of twelve countries that try to come up with common ideas about the environment, energy and farming in Europe.

How much rubbish do you throw away each week? Imagine how much rubbish all the people, shops and factories in Europe throw away each week! Or each year!

All the paper, glass, tins, boxes and plastic are collected and taken away. But where are they taken to?

Most of our rubbish is taken to dumps where machines crush it up. It is then put into holes in the ground and covered with soil. Sometimes the rubbish rots and produces a gas which pollutes the air. Rubbish is also burned and dumped in rivers and the sea.

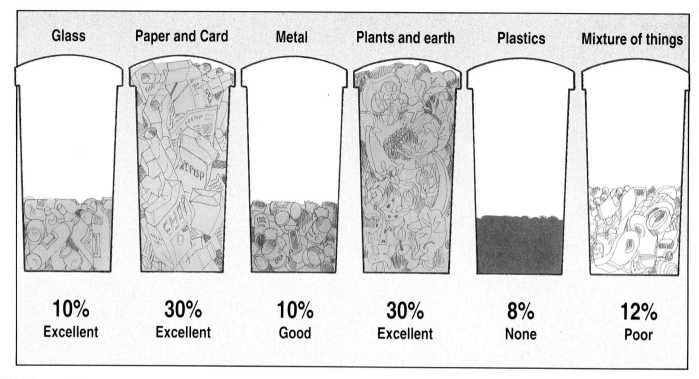

Glass	Paper and Card	Metal	Plants and earth	Plastics	Mixture of things
10% Excellent	**30%** Excellent	**10%** Good	**30%** Excellent	**8%** None	**12%** Poor

▲ *A lot of our rubbish can be recycled. This diagram shows which materials can be recycled.*

Some rubbish can be passed through special machines which grind and crush the rubbish. It can then be used as a fertilizer for soil.

◄ *This waste paper will be passed through machines which will make it into pulp. This can then be made into new paper.*

Venice

Tourists from all over the world flock to Venice in Italy every year. Many go to see the famous street canals.

However, this beautiful city has a lot of environmental problems.

Venice is built on a lagoon. This is a large pond that flows into the sea. The houses and buildings are built on wooden piles dug into the floor of the lagoon. Now these piles are rotting. This means the city is slowly sinking into the lagoon.

In the past, long, narrow boats called gondolas carried people around Venice. Today, power boats skim along the canals (above). These cause huge waves which also wear away the wooden piles.

Holidays and holidaymakers

People from all over the world visit Europe each year. Some ski in the mountains of France, Austria, Switzerland and Italy. Many lie on the beautiful beaches of the south of France, Portugal, Italy and Spain, soaking up the hot sun.

◀ *Every year, the number of skiers whizzing down the slopes of Europe's ski resorts grows. This has damaged the soil on many mountains.*

▲ *The seaside towns (resorts) of Spain became very popular with holidaymakers in the 1960s and 1970s. Huge hotels were built along the coast. Now the hotels tower over beaches packed with sunbathers.*

Holidays and holidaymakers in Europe have seriously affected the environment.

Blocks of hotels have been built in small villages in the mountains and on the coasts. Many are ugly and spoil the otherwise beautiful landscape. Many beaches in Europe are crowded and dirty.

▲ *These pretty flowers grow on the slopes of the Alps, a range of mountains in Switzerland. This area is a Swiss National Park.*

Many countries in Europe need tourism. It provides jobs and brings in a lot of money. However, as we have seen, tourism can harm the environment.

Italy, Switzerland and Austria have set up National Parks. These are special areas in the countryside, on mountains and in towns. They are protected by the governments of the countries.

Changing weather

Temperatures in Europe are rising. Yet winters are longer and colder and there are more storms and rainfall.

The changing weather is caused by the greenhouse effect (see page 12).

▼ *The greenhouse effect has caused more rainfall and more floods. The Netherlands has areas of low, flat land. These could soon be lost under water.*

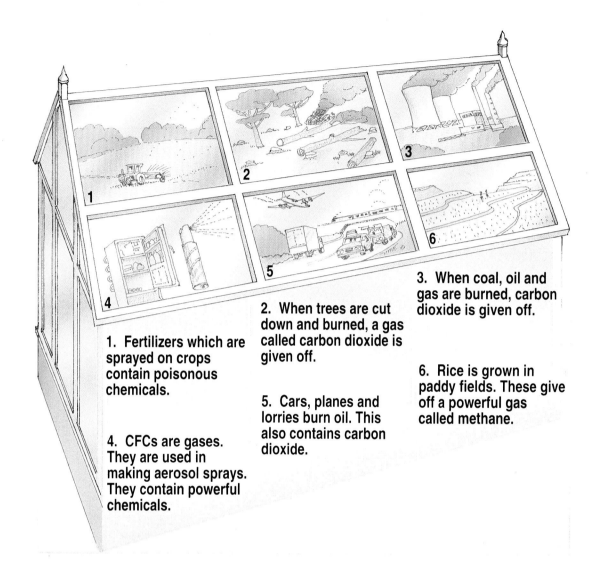

1. Fertilizers which are sprayed on crops contain poisonous chemicals.

2. When trees are cut down and burned, a gas called carbon dioxide is given off.

3. When coal, oil and gas are burned, carbon dioxide is given off.

4. CFCs are gases. They are used in making aerosol sprays. They contain powerful chemicals.

5. Cars, planes and lorries burn oil. This also contains carbon dioxide.

6. Rice is grown in paddy fields. These give off a powerful gas called methane.

The atmosphere (air) around the Earth stops harmful rays from the Sun (ultraviolet rays) reaching us.

But we are damaging the atmosphere. Smoke, fumes and chemicals are all polluting the air. They harm plants and animals and change the weather.

You have probably heard of the ozone layer.

Ozone is a gas found in the air. There is a layer of ozone above the surface of the Earth. This soaks up some of the heat from the Sun. It also helps to keep out harmful ultraviolet rays which can cause skin cancer and eye problems.

Large holes are appearing in the ozone layer. The damage is caused by pollution in the air from chemicals called chlorofluorcarbons, or CFCs. CFCs are used to make some aerosol sprays and hamburger cartons.

Many countries in Europe have banned the use of CFCs.

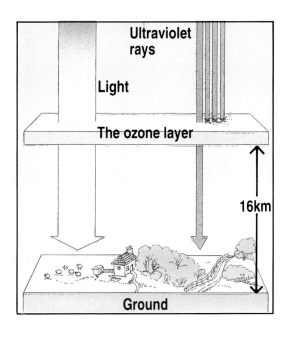

◀ *Damage to the ozone layer means that more harmful ultraviolet rays from the Sun reach the Earth.*

▲ *Be careful when sunbathing. Ultraviolet rays from the Sun can make people very ill.*

GREENPEACE

THE OZONE HOLE

Things are not getting better.
This year, the Antarctic ozone hole covered 14 million square kilometres, and the course is set for a new hole to appear over the Arctic. Meanwhile, governments are continuing to allow millions of tonnes of ozone destroying chemicals to be produced.

By linking scientific concern to public outrage, Greenpeace is campaigning to stop the production of all ozone destroyers – without delay.

THANK GOD SOMEONE'S MAKING WAVES

▲ *Greenpeace is an organization that tries to make people think more about the environment.*

▲ *Look at this green slime. It is algae – a type of seaweed caused by pollution.*

Holidaymakers once flocked to the beautiful sandy beaches of north-east Italy. Now these beaches are often thick with algae.

The future for the environment

▲ *This may look like a speed boat, but it is actually a car. It is powered by energy from the Sun.*

There are so many ways in which we are damaging the environment that it seems difficult to know where to begin or what to do.

If we do not do something, however, the greenhouse effect will get worse. Summers will be drier and hotter and winters will be colder and wetter. More wildlife will disappear. Fish and reptiles will die.

We must all try to help.

Governments could pass laws to stop factories and power-stations from causing pollution. Farmers could stop using chemicals on their crops.

People in Europe could recycle their waste. We could all pick up litter and keep our parks, towns and beaches tidy.

▼ *The environment in Europe is very beautiful. Let's make sure it stays that way.*

▲ *We must make sure that nature is not destroyed.*

The most important thing is to care about the environment.
It is very precious.

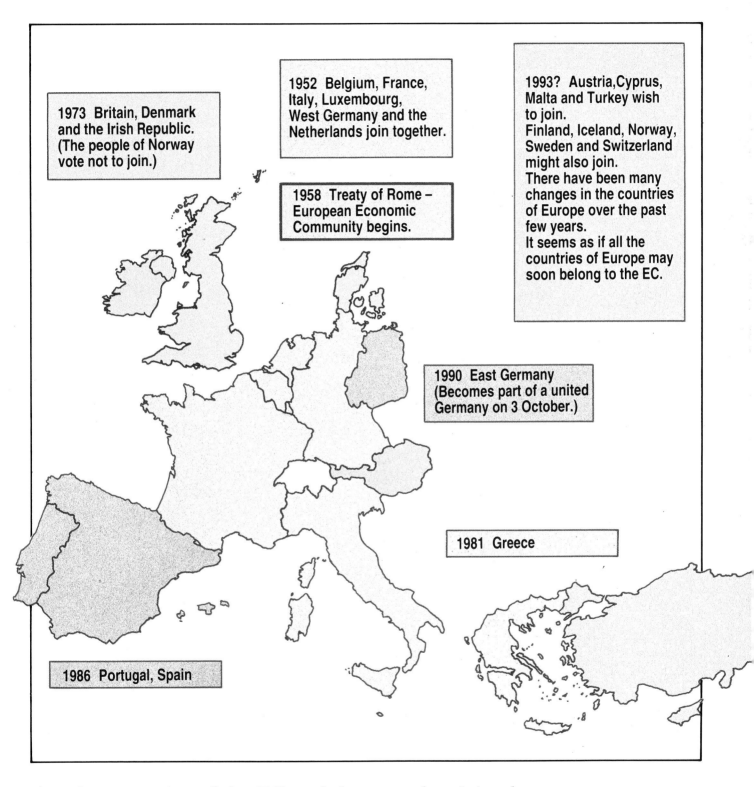

1973 Britain, Denmark and the Irish Republic. (The people of Norway vote not to join.)

1952 Belgium, France, Italy, Luxembourg, West Germany and the Netherlands join together.

1958 Treaty of Rome – European Economic Community begins.

1993? Austria, Cyprus, Malta and Turkey wish to join.
Finland, Iceland, Norway, Sweden and Switzerland might also join.
There have been many changes in the countries of Europe over the past few years.
It seems as if all the countries of Europe may soon belong to the EC.

1990 East Germany (Becomes part of a united Germany on 3 October.)

1981 Greece

1986 Portugal, Spain

▲ *The countries of the EC and the year they joined.*

Glossary

Car exhausts   The pipes from car engines which let out smoke.

Dams   Walls or banks of earth which are specially built to hold back water.

Filters   Machines which gases or liquids are passed through. The filters take out any dirt.

Fumes   Poisonous gases.

Landscape   The way in which the environment looks and its features, such as mountains, rivers, streams and valleys.

Lead   A heavy, grey metal.

Moisture   Slight wetness.

Peat   A type of soil which can be dried and used as fuel.

Poaching   To catch fish or hunt animals in areas where this is not allowed.

Pollution   Anything which harms the environment, such as smoke from power-stations and factory chimneys, poisonous chemicals and waste dumped in rivers or seas.

Pulp   The soft, moist mass of wood used for making paper.

Radiation   Dangerous rays of energy which are produced by the fuel in nuclear power-stations.

Recycled   When rubbish is passed through special machines which means it can be used again.

Waste   Something left over or not used.

Zinc   A bluish-white metal.

More information

Books to read

Acid Rain by Tony Hare (Franklin Watts, 1990)
Energy series (Wayland, 1993)
Ian and Fred's Big Green Book by Fred Pearce (Kingfisher, 1991)
Our Green World series (Wayland, 1991)
The Blue Peter Green Book by Lewis Bronze, Nick Heathcote and Peter Brown (BBC Books, 1990)
The Young Green Consumer Guide by John Elkington and Julia Hailes (Gollancz, 1990)

Further information

If you would like to find more information about the problems facing Europe's environment and what is being done to save it, you can write to these organizations.

Council of Europe
Boite Postale 431 R6
67006 Strasbourg Cedex
France

Earthscan
3 Endsleigh Street
London WC1H 0DD

Eurogeo
Geographical Institute
State University
Heidelberglaan 2
PO Box 80115
3508 TC Utrecht
Netherlands

Friends of the Earth
26-28 Underwood Street
London N1 7JQ

Greenpeace
Canonbury Villas
London N1 2PN

World Wide Fund for Nature
Panda House
Wayside Park
Godalming
Surrey GU7 1XR

Index